Welsbacher
Puerto Rico
32754

C-
972.95
Wy

DATE DUE

1948	

PRINTED IN U.S.A.

The United States

Puerto Rico

Anne Welsbacher
ABDO & Daughters

visit us at
www.abdopub.com

Published by Abdo & Daughters, 4940 Viking Drive, Suite 622, Edina, Minnesota 55435.
Copyright © 1998 by Abdo Consulting Group, Inc., Pentagon Tower, P.O. Box 36036,
Minneapolis, Minnesota 55435 USA. International copyrights reserved in all countries.
No part of this book may be reproduced in any form without written permission from the
publisher.

Printed in the United States.

Cover and Interior Photo credits: Peter Arnold, Inc., Archive, Corbis-Bettmann

Edited by Lori Kinstad Pupeza
Contributing editor Brooke Henderson
Special thanks to our Checkerboard Kids—Aisha Baker, Matthew Nichols, Raymond
Sherman, Francesca Tuminelly

All statistics taken from the 1990 census; The Rand McNally Discovery Atlas of The
United States.

Library of Congress Cataloging-in-Publication Data

Welsbacher, Anne
      Puerto Rico / Anne Welsbacher.
      p. cm. -- (United States)
      Includes index.
      Summary: Surveys the people, geography, and history of the Commonwealth of
      Puerto Rico.
      ISBN 1-56239-897-0
      1. Puerto Rico--Description and travel--Juvenile literature. [1. Puerto Rico.] I.
      Title. II Series: United States (Series)
      F1965.3.W4   1998
      972.95--dc21   97-40658
                                          CIP
                                          AC

Contents

Welcome to Puerto Rico

Puerto Rico is its own country, just like the United States! But it is very small. In many ways it is like a state. It is called a **commonwealth**.

Puerto Rico has many kinds of people. Some have lived there for a long time. Others came from Africa, Spain, and North America. Clothing, festivals, and customs are all a part of Puerto Rico's culture.

Puerto Rico has rain forests, seashores, and mountains. The land is very pretty. For this reason, Puerto Rico is called the Land of Enchantment.

Opposite page: Cabo Rojo
Lighthouse in Puerto Rico.

Fast Facts about the

COMMONWEALTH OF PUERTO RICO

Capital and largest city
San Juan (437,745 people)
Area
3,515 square miles
(9,104 sq km)
Population
3,522,037 people
Self-government granted
1917
Principal rivers
Grande de Anasco
Grande de Arecibo
Rio de la Plata
Highest point
Cerro de Punta;
4,389 feet (1,338 m)
Motto
Live free or die
Song
"La Borinquena"
Famous People
Juan "Chi Chi" Rodríguez,
Roberto Clemente, Sandy and
Roberto Alomar, José Feliciano,
José Ferrer, Rita Moreno

*N*ational Flag

*M*aga

*R*einita

*C*eiba

Commonwealth of Puerto Rico

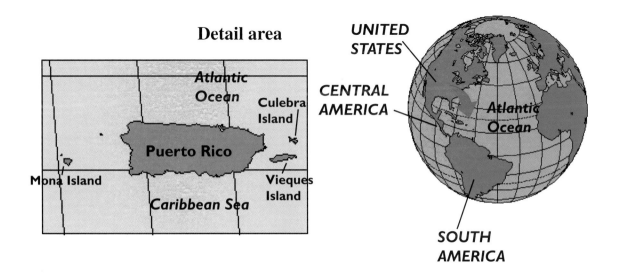

Borders: west (Mona water passage), north (Atlantic Ocean), east (Vieques water passage), south (Caribbean Sea)

Nature's Treasures

Puerto Rico's greatest treasure is its weather! All year long, the air is warm and not too dry. It never snows, but it rains almost every day. For this reason, many plants grow well in Puerto Rico.

The nice weather also draws many tourists. Water surrounds all of Puerto Rico. There are beautiful, sandy beaches.

The land contains clay, limestone, salt, sand, gravel, and stone. It also has nickel and copper. It once had gold, but the early Spanish explorers dug all the gold out of the ground.

Opposite page: A hiking trail in the Caribbean National Forest.

Beginnings

Native Americans were the first people to live on the island of Puerto Rico. By the year 1000, the **Taíno** (or "gentle") people lived there. They were sailors who traded with other islands and farmed.

The **Arawak** people lived on the island until the 1500s. They found gold on the island. They forced the native people to work in the gold mines and to farm on **plantations**. In 1493, Christopher Columbus claimed Puerto Rico for Spain. Spanish settlers arrived in 1508.

Soon, most of the native people died or left the island. Then slaves from Africa were forced to do the work. In the 1700s, many more **immigrants** came from Spain. More towns and plantations grew.

In the 1800s, slaves began to **rebel**. They wanted freedom. In 1873, the slaves from Africa were freed. And in 1898, Puerto Rico was given more **independence**.

In the same year, the United States won a war with Spain. Puerto Rico became a United States **Colony**.

Slowly, Puerto Rico won more rights from America. In 1917, Puerto Ricans became U.S. **citizens**. But unlike most citizens, Puerto Ricans could not vote for the president of the United States.

The 1930s were very hard times. Many people had no jobs. Two big **hurricanes** struck the island.

In 1952, Puerto Rico became a **commonwealth**, so it could be run by its own people. Many people moved to and from the United States. Many U.S. companies came to Puerto Rico.

Taíno Petroglyph Indian Ceremonial Center

Today, people talk and sometimes vote about their island's future. Should Puerto Rico become the 51st state? Should it stay a commonwealth? Or should it be a free country all on its own?

1000 to 1700s

Islanders

1000: **Taíno** people use boats to trade with other islands.

1508: The first settlers arrive from Spain. They bring diseases that kill most of the natives.

1700s: Many people arrive and build new towns and **plantations**.

Puerto Rico

1000 to 1700s

1868 to 1900s

Fighting for Freedom

1868: The people **rebel** in the town of Lares, demanding freedom.

1898: The United States takes over Puerto Rico after winning the Spanish American War.

1898-1900: The island is under military rule.

1917: Puerto Ricans become American **citizens.**

Puerto Rico

1868 to 1900s

1930s to Today

A Changing Country

1930s: Sugar and other crops are the biggest forms of making money. The United States begins to bring in companies to create new kinds of work.

1947: Puerto Ricans elect their own governor for the first time.

1993: Puerto Ricans vote to remain a **commonwealth**.

Puerto Rico

1930s to Today

Puerto Rico's People

There are 3.5 million people in Puerto Rico. Puerto Ricans are U.S. **citizens**, so they can come to America easily. They come to live in places near the island, like Florida.

Puerto Ricans have many backgrounds. Some are Hispanic. That means their long-ago families came from Spain. Others are a mix of Latino or African.

Rita Moreno was born in Puerto Rico. She is a famous actor, dancer, and singer. Actor José Ferrer, who starred in many plays, movies, and TV shows, also was from Puerto Rico. And singer José Feliciano was born in Puerto Rico.

The great baseball player Roberto Clemente was from Puerto Rico. Clemente also was a great **humanitarian**. He died in a plane crash while helping earthquake victims.

Other people born in Puerto Rico include golf great Juan "Chi Chi" Rodríguez, gold-medal winner Beatriz "Gigi" Fernández, and the Alomar baseball family, Sandy Sr., Sandy Jr., and Roberto.

"Chi Chi" Rodríguez

Roberto Clemente

Rita Moreno

Puerto Rico's Cities

San Juan is the largest city in Puerto Rico. It also is the capital of Puerto Rico. It is near the ocean, and ships come and go.

Outside of San Juan is the next largest city, Bayamón. The third largest city is Ponce.

Other cities are Carolina and Mayagüez. Mayagüez is on the west coast of the island.

Opposite page: San Juan, Puerto Rico.

Puerto Rico's Land

Puerto Rico began under the sea! Volcanoes blew and earthquakes shook. Land below the ocean rose up and formed Puerto Rico and other islands.

Puerto Rico is short and wide. It is only 35 miles (56 km) from north to south. If the land was flat, it would take less than one hour to drive that far!

Most of Puerto Rico's land is rocky hills, slopes, and mountains. Only a small percentage of the land is level. Because of the rugged land, not too many areas are good for farming.

In the middle of the country are high mountains. Coffee and fruit are grown in this area. On both sides of the mountains are smaller hills.

Smaller Hills

35 Miles

Rugged Mountains

Smaller Hills

Some areas in Puerto Rico get a lot of rain. Just north of the mountains it rains on the average of 80 to 120 inches (200 to 300 cm) a year! Other areas, however, are very dry.

Along the coasts are many beaches and little bays. Near the north and south shores are lowlands. Here sugar cane is grown.

Once most of the island was a tropical rain forest. Now most of the forests are gone. But many pretty trees still grow. Some are the **flamboyan**, with big red blossoms, or the African tulip. Some trees grow foods like papayas, sea grapes, or star apples.

Most of Puerto Rico is mountainous.

Puerto Ricans at Play

Songs and dances from African and Latino cultures mix together to make music in Puerto Rico. The music is played on drums, **maracas**, and other instruments.

Puerto Ricans celebrate many holidays, both from the United States and from their own country. They dance, make music, and dress in bright, colorful costumes.

The June feast of San Juan Bautista lasts for a week. Families go to the beach, eat tasty treats, and listen to **salsa** music.

On September 23, Puerto Ricans celebrate Grito de Lares. That is the day, in 1868, that people living in the town of Lares fought for their freedom.

Baseball is a much-loved sport. Puerto Rican ball players are in both American and island league teams. Their fans can watch baseball almost every day!

Puerto Ricans enjoy relaxing in cafes. Many nights, concerts are played on street corners—by both grown-ups and children!

Puerto Ricans visit the Coamo spa where hot springs shoot warm water out of the ground all year long. They go to the beaches or hike in the mountains. And they also enjoy riding horses and surfing in the ocean waves.

Puerto Ricans have many beaches to visit.

Puerto Ricans at Work

Many Puerto Ricans work in **manufacturing**. They make medicine and tools to use in science. Puerto Ricans also work at the places tourists go, like motels, shops, and places to eat.

Once many people farmed. But today farming is only a small part of the work Puerto Ricans do. Farmers grow sugarcane, coffee beans, and many fruits, like pineapples, bananas, and coconuts.

Many times it is hard to find work. Looking for work is one reason people travel between the island and the United States. Creating more work for Puerto Rico is a problem that both countries are trying to solve.

Opposite page: Lots of pineapples are grown in Puerto Rico.

Fun Facts

- The town of San Juan was first called "Puerto Rico" by the early Spanish settlers. (*Puerto Rico* is Spanish for "rich port.") Later the name spread to mean the whole island.
- Cactus plants grow in Puerto Rico! They are in the Guánica Dry Forest near Ponce. Many kinds of trees and birds also grow and live in the forest.
- An old legend says that anyone who sees the shy coquí frog while it sings will have good luck.
- Puerto Rico has so many holidays that shops close about two times every month to celebrate!
- The flavors put into Coca-Cola and Pepsi are made in Cidra, a town in Puerto Rico.
- Some favorite foods and drinks in Puerto Rico are made from coconuts, pigs, and a firm kind of banana

called a plantain (PLAN-tan). Coco frío (KO-ko FREE-o) is cold coconut milk in a coconut shell. Lechón asado (LAY-chon a-SAW-do) is roast pig, served for holidays. Fritters are fried pieces of plantain. Some of the other fruits enjoyed by Puerto Ricans are the custard apple, the quenepa (koo-eh-NEH-pah), and the hog plum.

The coqui frog can bring good luck to a Puerto Rican.

Glossary

Arawak: people who once lived on Puerto Rico.
Citizen: a member of a country.
Colony: a place owned by another country.
Commonwealth: a country or state run by its own people.
Flamboyan: a kind of tree that grows in Puerto Rico.
Greater Antilles Islands: a string of islands southeast of Florida; they are named Hispaniola (which has Haiti and the Dominican Republic), Jamaica, Cuba, and Puerto Rico.
Humanitarian: someone who helps other people.
Hurricane: a big storm that begins over water.
Immigrant: a person who moves to a country from another country.
Independence: freedom.
Manufacture: to make things.
Maraca: a musical instrument that makes a soft cha-cha sound when shaken; it is made from a pumpkin-like plant that is dried and has its insides taken out, and then is filled with stones or dried beans.
Plantation: a big farm.
Rebel: to fight back against a rule or a way of doing things.
Salsa: a kind of music special to Puerto Rico; it has a strong beat, and is played with a special kind of drum made from sticks.
Taíno: people who once lived on Puerto Rico.

Internet Sites

Puerto Rico Boriken
http://users.aol.com/np4cc/puertori.htm
This site is colorful and interactive with both sound and animation. It comes in both Spanish and English. Learn about the island's history, national symbols, places to see, weather, and much more.

El Paraiso De Edgardo
http://ww2.esn.net/~boricua/
Come and listen to different kinds of music that are enjoyed in Puerto Rico. This site is really cool. You can pick the style of music you want, then you get a library of songs to hear. Also, the whole site is in Spanish, which is always fun!

These sites are subject to change. Go to your favorite search engine and type in Puerto Rico for more sites.

PASS IT ON

Tell Others Something Special About Your State

To educate readers around the country, pass on interesting tips, places to see, history, and little unknown facts about Puerto Rico or the state you live in. We want to hear from you!

To get posted on ABDO & Daughters website, e-mail us at "mystate@abdopub.com"

Index